Gujarati

Wedding

Planner

Checklist

Importance of rituals

Execution of events

Author

Divya Parikh

Copyright

Acknowledgement

I Acknowledge the input of my mother Dr. Bina Shah for explaining all the rituals performed in a Hindu wedding very patiently and also helping me in editing this book.

Special thanks to my selfless supporters - my Daughter Vishwa – 4 years old and Son Harshil - 1 year old for giving me time to write this book and to my husband Nilay for giving me challenges which I love to fulfill.

Journey to this Book

Wedding is an event which every parent dreams about when the child is born. It is the longest awaited event. Can you not make it flawless and tension free by proper planning?

The feeling of regret of not being able to do something in the wedding which you wished to do, due to lack of planning or mismanagement, is very haunting. It hurts you for long. So to avoid any regrets, I thought we should have a checklist in hand which takes care of all macro and micro planning of the events. When planned in advance there are less chances of missing anything.

When a wedding date is decided, my mother and my mother-in-law usually receives phone calls of relatives to discuss about what to do and what not to do in a wedding as they are elders, and they have recent experiences.

It was the same thing my mother did during my wedding. She discussed everything with her mother. But just thinking about my future 25 years down, for my daughter and son's wedding, a thought sparked, how about having everything in written format so that it becomes very easy for me and thousands of people like me to plan a wedding single handedly?

Moreover, basic rituals and points to keep in mind while planning the event are not going to change for years to come so if I have a checklist of things to be done, it would turn out to be a great help to me and others. Hence got an idea to write a book and document it so it would be helpful to make decisions to make wedding a great memorable event of life.

Divya Parikh
May 2024

Index

My heartiest congratulations to you for deciding your life partner. You must now be dreaming about the D Day when you both will be tied in a knot and your families will be connected with a relationship. You must now be a little excited and tense as well, to plan all the activities so that the entire wedding rituals, starting from engagement to reception become memorable for you and for all the invited guests.

I will provide you with all the details of macro and micro planning needed to execute the wedding ceremonies, single handedly.

This book is your best choice to release tension at the last moment and help you enjoy the moments yourself.

There are various verticals to plan and execute, while planning a wedding. We will go through it in detail one by one.

Primary Preparations

When the engagement is declared you may arrange Gol dhana function or engagement ring ceremony function. In Gol- dhana function the bride's mother and family go to the groom's place, give a shrifal and one rupee coin and whatever gift you wish to give to groom in groom's hand by doing a tilak on his forehead. Same way Groom's mother gives gift to bride. One elder person declares that daughter of so and so person is engaged for wedding with son of so and so person.Then both the families have lunch together and depart.

After the engagement ceremony discuss with bride/groom's family and get 2 to 3 optional dates for wedding after discussion with brahmin, convey the same to the bride/groom family and finalize one date and time for wedding convenient to both bride and groom family. Usually this is done 4 to 5 months earlier to get venue booking of choice.

Things to keep in mind while finalizing the date:

1. Make sure in case of cancellation other muhurat is available.

2. Check if it's possible to get a Saturday or a Sunday for the wedding date or reception date so that maximum guests can come.

3. If you need to keep other functions before or after wedding date, please select the wedding day accordingly.

4. Cross check the availability of hall (venue) in which you wish to do the wedding and other functions.

5. The date should not be such that too many weddings are there on that date or else

your guests will be divided, for example Vasant Panchami, Akha trij etc.

After deciding the date, the basic events you need to plan in a wedding are:

1. Ring ceremony

2. Pagla padvanu

3. Vadi Papad

4. Kankotri writing

5. Path/Vivah khel

6. Mehndi

7. Bachelor party

8. Mandap muhurat

9. Ganesh sthapan

10. Grah Shanti

11. Pithi /Haldi

12. Sangeet

13. Wedding

14. Pag phero

15. Reception

There may be differences in rivaj/customs of wedding in different castes and religion, you may modify accordingly, but the basic planning for those functions remains the same. Some of the requirements of items and things may change.

Once this is decided, think of the venue.

1. Destination wedding

2. Same city wedding

3. Different cities wedding (taking barat)

For the destination wedding you may have to take help of an event manager to find and coordinate with different local agencies. For 2 and 3 I am providing every detail to conduct the functions without the help of event manager with equal accuracy.

Fix an approximate budget for your wedding. Classify your budget on broad headings like, apparels, jewelry, gifts, beautyparlour, photography and wedding/reception/functions. Your budget will have 10% increment at the end of the event.

Calculate the approximate number of invitees as you will have to select the venue according to its capacity.

Invitee List

First make a basic list of invitees in a paper or a diary with space for columns beside it. Then if possible, convert that list into an excel sheet to make it more precise.

First start from the relatives.

From Father's side and Mother's side

1. Kaka
2. Mama
3. Foi
4. Masi
5. First cousin, second cousins
6. Sons and daughters of cousins

Confirm the names of the family member's with your elders.

Then comes the friend circle of Mother, Father, Bride/ Groom and sibling.

Then professional circle of Mother, Father, Bride/ groom and the Siblings.

Also make a list of various other groups in which your family members are involved. It can be your neighbours, clientele, Club organizations, suppliers etc. with whom you have social relationship.

Keep few blank spaces to add names as and when you recall, so new list is not to be made.

Only one list needs to be kept edited.

Make different columns as per your events.

Add the number of persons to be invited from the same family in the event which you want.

This single list will be helpful in giving you information about how many kankotris to be printed, if you have many events then how to distribute the numbers of flaps of kankotris to adjust all events and all invitees. This list will also provide you with numbers of persons for lunch, dinner and breakfast, snacks etc. on each event day for which you have to make provision. So this list is very important. You write the names of family head with pen and **number of persons in pencil** so that you can edit easily. This list will also give you information about how many people to take in jaan. This list will be the backbone of your catering, jaan, and kankotri.

Family head's Name	Kankotri Ph.no	Baraat	Accomodation	Transport	Event 1	Event 2
			A	T	B M S E	B M S E

In the above table you write down the list of all your invitees. Use different pages for your different categories of invitees. Under the heading of Kankotri you mention either you have to give E invite or hard copy. If E-invite then write His phone no. At the same time you tick mark for which function you have to invite them. Under M and E you write the numbers of guests you have to invite in the morning for lunch or evening for dinner and under B for breakfast and under S for snacks, under A for accodomation (if you have to provide), under T for transport (if you have to provide) respectively. Make columns of every events wherein you have to provide catering e.g.mehndi, sangeet, vivah khel, grahshanti, baraat, wedding, reception, other times when nos. are less but you have to provide meals to guests etc.

For kankotri, if you have different guests for different events then write G for grahshanti, S for sangeet, J for jaan, W for wedding and R for reception against their name under Kankotri. Write GSJWR against family's head name who has to be invited for all events. This way you will get the list of S, J, W, R and the total of which will help you in utilizing the flaps accordingly.

When this list is ready you write down the total at the end of column in each page. Now it will be very easy to find out total numbers for each item, it may be M, E, B, S for all events, A , Baraat, Kankotri and T for outstation guests.

If it's destination wedding make allotment of guests in respective rooms.

Once the dates and invitee list is decided you will have nos. of guests in hand, the next step will be Venue survey as per your nos. of guests. It can be a banquet, lush green lawn or a resort.

Venue Booking

Things you should keep in mind while doing the survey are:

1. It should be near to your house.
2. Decide whether you want to keep it in open or close. It will depend on the season and the temperature, In winter it is okay to keep in an open lawn where as in summer it is advisable to go for a closed AC banquet hall.
3. Select a venue which has both hall and lawn because of non-seasonal unexpected rains.
4. Venue rent should match your budget.
5. Find out who is the decorator of the hall.
6. Find out who is the caterer of the hall and how is the food.
7. Find out if you can select your own decorator and caterer.
8. Check the quality, neatness and cleanliness of the hall/lawn.

9. Check the lawn quality whether it is maintained or not or else you will have to add green carpet.
10. Check the entry direction and the driveway from main road.
11. Check the parking capacity of the hall/lawn, how many cars can be accommodated along with two wheelers.
12. Does it have a bride and groom's room and how many extra rooms are there?
13. Check the Chori location where it can be and whether It is seen from all directions or not.
14. Check the capacity of the hall/lawn, how many guests it can accommodate, does it match your approximate invitee list?
15. Check how many chairs can be placed around the Chori and what is the sitting capacity of the guests.
16. Check out the dining area and how big or small it is? It should not get overcrowded after placing round tables with chair. Maximum crowding you will get during meal hours. This space should accommodate atleast 50% of the invitees at a time.
17. Check the catering arrangement. Where will be the tables placed and how the food will be served on the counters from the back kitchen?
18. Check what all the things need to be decorated as it will cost you.

19. If your wedding time is in the evening, then check the shadow pattern. Will overhead covering be needed?
20. Check the walkway length for decoration, it should not be too long nor too short.
21. Check the neatness and cleanliness of the people as well as the washroom, that will tell you the meticulousness of the owner.
22. After talking to the owner check the flexibility and adjustment capacity of the owner in case of any changes as per your requirement.
23. Discuss with the owner, if by chance in case of any cancellation what are the pros and cons of it.
24. Finalize an approximate costing of the venue.
25. Ask the owner to show the photographs of the event held at the venue.
26. Visit a function at the same Hall or lawn when it is live, so you can get the perfect idea of your event.

After comparing 3 to 4 halls finalize which suits you best. Once convinced, confirm the hall and give the booking amount. Write everything discussed with the owner in your own diary so you don't forget and you have a record of your discussion.

Next step is to confirm venue for other occasions. Things to keep in mind while deciding would be the same points as above. Either you can book the same Hall or lawn or find another place, or you can do it in front of your house. If in case you are planning a few events in front of your house or in your society, club house or common plot, the basic things to keep in mind are as follows.

1. Number of people who are invited for the event should be accommodated easily.
2. Finalize the decorator and the caterer who will be handling your event.
3. There should be enough parking space for the invited guests.
4. Decide how much area will you be enclosing and also decide the place for entry.
5. Plan the placement of the activities where you will do the pooja, which would be the dining area, where will be the tables of the catering and how much to cover above and sides.
6. Check the natural light in the day and plan the lighting and halogen locations for night accordingly.
7. Decide whether you want to cover the floor with the carpet or not.
8. Find out how many standing fans and coolers will you need if your event is in summer and gas heaters in case of winters.
9. Decide the Place for Drinking water, washing hands and used plate to keep the place neat and clean at the time of event.
10. Finalize the colour of the fabric and jhul to be used to cover the area.

Now once the hall/lawn is booked, list of invitees and time of every event are finalized, we need to approach other agencies to fix their date and time with us in order to coordinate well.

The list is

1. Photographer
2. Kankotri printer
3. Decorator
4. Caterer
5. Beauty parlour
6. Brahmin
7. Bus booking if required
8. Mehndi wala
9. Dholi
10. Matliwala/kumbhar
11. Valley parking
12. Band/dj booking
13. Car decoration
14. Ghodi if required
15. Choreographer
16. Anchor of event
17. Instrumental musician in wedding if required

We will now get into the detail of what all to discuss and clarify with the respective agencies, along with finalizing the date and the total amount.

Caterer

Shortlist 3 to 4 good caterers and visit their event and taste the food. Check live counters, display, Ambience and cleanliness of the space.

Things to discuss with caterer are:

1. Discuss the date, time and location of the event and also what time you need the food ready.
2. Discuss the packages as per your budget. Get the menu card from him and decide the main menu of wedding and reception and for other events as per your choice. While deciding the menu do not forget to add side items like papad, salads, chutneys, fryums, mukhvas etc.
3. See that mostly food items are not repeated so people get variety to eat.
4. Discuss the number of serving tables he will keep to serve invitees.
5. Discuss the requirements of caterer through decorator, so that there is no hustle at the last moment e.g. serving tables for different counters, live stations etc.
6. Have a look at the crockery they will be serving food in the live station and main course.

Decorator

Decorator plays an important role in creating the Ambience of the whole wedding and working with the psychology of the guest so it is very important to have an excellent decorator as 60 to 70% role is of decorator in the wedding to make it memorable.

So survey few different decorators and if the decorator is fixed then confirm the dates, day and timings of different events with him and check his availability for different events. Confirm the location for each event.

There are packages offered in decoration, so see the photos of different packages and select few which you like. Get in detail of all those packages, what do they offer.

Things to be decorated at the lawn/hall are

1. Entry Gate with a welcome Note, with the name of bride and groom and the invitee family.
2. Walkway and the pathway leading to the main event area.
3. Chori in case of wedding and reception stage in case of reception.
4. Given the number of invitees, discuss the seating arrangement of chairs and sofa in front of chori/reception stage. The chair needs to be covered with two colour fabric.

5. The Dining counters and the dining area needs to be decorated either with jhul or MDF screen. Special artifacts which are eye catching can be placed with item tags at the counter.
6. General Party Plot lighting should be done with every area lit up with halogens and all the surrounding trees needs to be highlighted with bottom focus lights or either with series.
7. Keep in mind for the Provision of generator.
8. Discuss the height of the stage or the chori such that it is visible from every location.
9. Check the live photos of the chori and the reception stage and select the one which you like, and tell him that it should be exactly the same.
10. The steps to climb the reception stage should be sturdy and wide.
11. Clarify the use of fresh flowers or artificial flowers wherever necessary as fresh flowers will cost you a lot.
12. Discuss whether they will be placing fountains in between or not.
13. If you wish a special customize theme discuss the requirement with decorator.
14. There should be provision of light point plugs at different locations as required.
15. In case of winter season discuss if heaters are available or not and in case of summers see the availability of coolers.

16. If in case there is any other idea in your mind discuss it clearly with the decorator.
17. All the wedding related items - 2 chairs , 2 bajot , hawan kund etc should be provided by decorator
18. There should be two people specially alloted to keep the place neat and clean, picking up the plastic bottles and any other filth thrown on floor/lawn.

Brahmin

He is generally required for Ganesh Sthapan, Mandap Muhurat, Grah Shanti and wedding(bride side) so discuss all the timings with him.

1. The start time of the pooja.
2. The total time which he will require to complete the pooja.
3. Also clear what all items will be required for every event and get a list of those items in detail including everything- event wise from him.
4. Clarify if we need to bring or if he is going to bring those things.
5. If it's partial then clarify the list with Brahmin, what he will bring and what we need to provide e.g. pooja samagri, kunds, bajot, matli etc.
6. Understand the full process so we get clarity of what will we be doing there in every event as per your system in your caste.

Photographer

Photographer plays the most important role in whole of the wedding ceremony because he is the person who will show you how your wedding event was celebrated. You would be too busy to get a glimpse of the arrangement and to meet the arrived guests. By photography you can relive the wedding as many times you want.

To finalise a photographer, do a survey of 3 to 4 photographers, check the images and reviews of clients who have worked with them.

Things to discuss with them:

1. Brief him the location of different events along with the date and time of the event which are to be photographed by him.
2. Check their availability for the same date and time and also discuss about the backup team.
3. See the albums sample made by them.
4. Also see short films samples edited by them.

Once you are convinced, go ahead for a detailed discussion.

1. Confirm him the number of photographers who will come for the shoot.
2. There should be One photographer for chori and other one or two photographers

to take Candid photos of guest so there is a complete coverage of invitees.
3. There should be one video grapher and one helper with him at the Chori.
4. Ask him if he is providing a Drone and how they will operate.
5. In case of reception do you want a crane ?

Tell them timings of half an hour before the actual timings as they need time to set up their lights, cameras etc .

Confirm the approximate time required for personal photo shoot so you can adjust that time in your wedding time table.

In case you are also planning a Pre wedding photo shoot, things you should discuss are:

1. Convey your selected locations and discuss the timings of shoot for the best quality of pictures, either sunset or sunrise. Check if you have to take permission of the place to photograph.
2. Clarify who will bring the appropriate props and clothings required for photoshoot.
3. The Location should have the availability of changing room and resting room.
4. Decide who all will be coming - a photographer, drone or a videographer

Now also get the clarity of the album, short film and the raw images.

1. Confirm the album size which would be printed, with number of pages in it.
2. Clarify the types of pages- whether a plastic print, matt finish or glossy finish, thickness of pages, number of photographs to be accomodated and weather it would be hard bound or soft Bound.
3. For short films discuss the approximate time duration of the video and finally freeze the budget.

Photographer needs to come at home first for family photos and then to the event location.

Family needs to be ready half an hour prior to the decided time to enjoy the portrait and group photo shoot with bride/ groom.

Personal photos of bride and groom take lot of time, so discuss the timings with them and adjust the same accordingly in your wedding time table.

Beauty parlour

In case of discussing for beauty parlour make sure you get a very positive review from other clients and also discuss the products which they will be using for the makeup so that it is skin friendly, it should not create any side effect on your face. A trial before can help you to decide your look as per your choice.

Tell her you need a decent and an elegant look.

Things to discuss with the beauty parlour person are:

1. Convey the dates, timings and events to finalise their availability.
2. Convey the time at which you need to be ready for the event, that is Ganesh, grah Shanti, Sangeet, wedding and reception.
3. It needs to be one hour prior the start timing of the event as you have to keep buffer time to reach at the destination and also for portrait photoshoot.
4. Ask for what all she will be providing - Facial, medicure, pedicure, nail art, hair styling, makeup, wearing saree and lehenga etc.
5. Discuss about the pre wedding facial trials she will be giving and approximately how many days before.
6. Show her your dresses prior the event, so she can arrange your matching Broach and hair decoration accessories which is required.
7. Ask for the time she will require to make you ready, so confirm the start time for beauty parlour accordingly.
8. Get a trial hairstyling and makeup 15 days prior to event to finalise the wedding day

look, so there is no confusion on wedding day.

Mehndi wala

Finalize the number of people invited in mehndi and calculate the approximate hands that would be putting Mehndi- front and back.

Convey the date and time of the event and finalize the rate of each hand. Ask her to write the name of the person and number of hands, to make the final payment.

For bride and the mother, finalize the rate and time to keep mehndi, also confirm how long it will take to keep mehndi, so that you can plan your lunch/dinner accordingly.

Use natural mehndi so that there is no reaction on the skin later on.

Choreographer

Once it is decided to do a Sangeet function together, (bride and groom) a choreographer is hired to make the function professional and memorable. Take the reference of the choreographer from his previous clienteles.

Things to keep in mind while deciding with him

1. Convey the date and start time of the event.
2. Give a clear idea about the theme of the sangeet event.
3. Give him the time duration of whole event and number of participants so that he can design the whole event. If possible, ask him to remain present in the event.
4. Plan the sequence of dances and convey the sequence to the participants clearly to avoid any hustle.

Bus Booking

Finalize the number of people who will be coming by bus as per your list in baraat.

One seat for each person, so book the bus accordingly either 32 seater or 56 seater or two buses as per your budget.

Inform all the baratis to arrive half an hour before your scheduled time to leave. The scheduled time will be decided keeping in mind the time for photography and pooja vidhi.

Bus should be neat and clean with AC. AC should be started half an hour before the leaving time.

Get permissions if required to bring the bus to a specific location.

Decide the location of bus pickup point and drop off point, so there is no issue of the parking.

Kankotri printing

Kankotri is basically a hard copy invitation sent to all invitees so that they remember the date.

Now a days even an E Kankotri is sent on whatsapp in far land and then a call is made.

So while printing the Kankotri the things to keep in mind are:

1. Calculate the number of families from the guest list to whom kankotri is to be sent so that you get the number of kankotris to be printed.
2. Check the decency and elegance of kankotri. Try to select light base colour so that the write up is clearly visible. Write up is generally red in colour.
3. Check the proof reading twice and it's spacing in your page size.

Now before finalizing the printing matter, you need to be very clear with your wedding time table.

Your wedding time table should include the beauty parlour timing, photography timing, transportation timing and the actual Pooja timing. So make a tentative wedding time table including all these timings and then finalize the time of the event.

Kankotri should contain different flaps for different events

Flap 1 - Mandap Muhrat / Ganesh sthapan / Grah Shanti / mameru

Flap 2 - Sangeet

Flap 3 - Jaan prasthan / hast melap /wedding

Flap 4 - Reception

Flap 5 - Mehndi / pithi

So in every kankotri only respective flaps should go in which you want to invite that person. So you need to calculate the number of flaps for every event from your invitee list.

Things which should be written very clearly in the flaps are

1. Event name
2. Date , day , time , dinner time / lunch time of respective event
3. Venue of respective event
4. Name of the bride and groom with parents and other elders.

Your cover page should include the name of bride and groom, date, day, time of the event, venue and invitee's name so that one doesn't need to open the kankotri. Only by looking the cover page one recalls that one has to go in this event.

On the day of kankotri writing, sit with a list of invitees bifurcated as per their relation and having addresses with it.

You can be specific whether 1/2/ full family members whom you wish to invite. That's completely your choice.

Dholi

Dholi is generally required during Ganesh Matli, gruhshanti and Mameru, also during Jan prasthan

So finalize the time with him accordingly. Also finalize the rate and how many people will come - 2 or 3.

Car decoration

If the groom is coming by car then the car needs to be decorated. Choose the bouquet you like and finalize the rate. Also confirm the timing by which you want it to be ready.It should be ready half an hour before the Jaan prasthan or baraat.

Valet Parking

Valet parking is generally required in wedding and reception. Also keep in mind the parking facility at other locations of your events. Decide if you require there also or not.

Ask him to keep the total count of the cars in written with car numbers to make the final payment.

Convey the date and timings of the event and finalize the rate.

Ghodi/elephant/bagi

Book a Ghodi/elephant/bagi or any vehicle for groom to ride on for baraat, seeing the photos of the decoration and finalize the rate. Convey him the location and time half an hour before the baraat time.

Safawala

Search the safawala on client review.

1. Convey the date and timings of baraat and finalize the rate.
2. Decide the approximate total number of safa you need.
3. Confirm how many numbers of people will come to tie safa as it will take time. It should be done in half an hour maximum.

4. Assign one person from house to collect all safa after baraat reaches the mandap so they are not misplaced.
5. Decide the design and colour of safa from pictures.

Band or DJ booking

Convey the date and timings of baraat and finalize the rate.

1. Hear a small clipping of the band and get a review from his clients.
2. Clarify with him if a DJ will be coming or a singer or a team of instruments will be coming.
3. Clarify how many people will come and what will be the dress code of people.
4. Decide the location point of the Baraat, where it will be starting and for how much time it will be played.

Crackers

Buy the crackers for the baraat and assign the responsibility to a young person of your family to bring them at the place of baraat. Ask him to take along with him a matchbox or taramandal to light it.

It is advisable to buy the crackers during Diwali time to get it at reasonable rates.

Shopping

This topic is completely left on you as this is a personal topic and it depends on your choices and how much you wish to spend on clothes and jewelry. But please plan the budget and the necessities.

Finalize the dress of every event with symbolic colour of your choice along with the jewelry related to the dress.

If you are thinking of gifting items at different events, that is in grahshanti or vivah khel or return gifts then select those items as per your choice and budget.

Now let's go through every event in detail. Here I have explained all rituals as per vaishnav gnyati but there may be few variations. Consult your elders for that.

Vadi papad

1. Take 750gms of chola ni dal and soak it overnight. Crush it in a mixture jar with salt, Adu, mirchi. Keep the paste ready in one big bowl. Divide the content into five small bowls so that each one gets one bowl.
2. Place one big plastic sheet on the floor, draw a swastika with kanku in the centre, shower akshat(rice) and flowers and start putting vadi. Do the same for papad.
3. Buy 25 to 30 Papad gulas for the event. Keep ready five orasiya, five velan and 5 aasans on which people will sit. One big plastic should be placed on the floor to put the papad. Keep ready some oil in small bowl to put it on orasiya.
4. Play background music of lagna geet to create an ambience.
5. Put chairs around to see the event who cannot sit down.
6. If the event is at home, decorate the house with basic fresh flowers or decoration material would add charm to the ambience.

Chola dal signifies shukan. Vadi papad is said to be the beginning of marriage. It is usually done on the day of Kankotri writing i.e 20-25 days before marriage date. Papads are then distributed to kutumb's family as a gesture to inform about the marriage in advance and that you are important to us.

Kankotri Writing

1. Keep the printed kankotri handy in different piles so it is easy to write.
2. Keep the list of invitees and their addresses ready.
3. Do Swastik on 1st kankotri with kanku, shower Akshat(rice) and flowers, and write God's name as the first invitee.
4. First five or 11 kankotris need to be written to gods and offered to different Temples, then in laws, then elders of the family and the list goes on.
5. Play background music of Lagna geet to give a wedding ambience and put chairs around to see who cannot sit on the floor.
6. Keep sweets and snacks handy to share after the writing is completed.
7. If it is followed by lunch or dinner, convey that to the guests prior.
8. If any return gifts are to be given then keep those ready.

Kankotri is a document of invitation. It is then distributed to the invitees personally. When given personally it represents the warmth of relationships, your contacts are renewed and you get their blessings. You also get confirmation of their attending the marriage. It is usually believed that once kankotri distribution starts the host will not attend any funerals or Besana. The reason being that the excitement of the host should not be disturbed.

Path/ vivah khel

1. Decide the number of people to be invited and set the sitting arrangement accordingly as they are going to sit at one place for 3 hours.
2. Consider people sitting down and on chair and plan accordingly.
3. Check the decoration part around the deity to be kept and make it beautiful.
4. Kanku, Chokha, fresh flowers, Prasad etc should be kept ready.
5. If you wish to sing special songs, keep the Xerox of it ready so all can sing it in chorus.
6. If you wish to give any return gifts then keep it ready.
7. In case of need of a music system, keep ready 2-3 mics with proper location of speakers.
8. In case of open area, it should be covered from top and specific sides to enclose it. Make arrangements of fans or coolers depending on time and season. Floor must have green carpet.

9. After the event gets completed, there should be provision of hot milk and Prasad. Heavy snacks or dinner can be planned.
10. Water should be served in between, to avoid dryness of throat.

Path or Vivah khel is organized a day or two before the wedding day. This is done to invoke God for successful completion of the whole event.

Mehndi

1. In case of mehndi for bride there should be a proper seat comfortable to her, with a small table to put her feet on it and cushions and waste clothes should be available at the place. It should be comfortable for the mehndi wala also to put mehndi.
2. In case you are making it a big function please add some music system with proper speaker arrangement as per the location. You tube can help you play event specific songs.
3. Coordinate the timings with the photographer to have a complete coverage of mehndi function.
4. 2 or 3 pillows should be there with each person keeping mehndi along with the waste clothes to make it comfortable and keep it neat and clean.

5. If in case one wish to put Nilgiri tel then it should be available.
6. Juice or water or any drink should be served in between followed by dinner.
7. In case of performance, a special stage with specific decoration of fresh flowers should be made to make it decent and elegant.

Applying Mehndi on bride's palms and legs is an ancient tradition in almost all religions. Mehndi imparts red color to the skin thus making it very attractive. This keeps bride's and all other's mood elevated and atmosphere of joy is created.

Sangeet

Now coming to one main function of the wedding where the number of people are more from both side the bride and the groom.

The main invitee has to decide theme, maybe from bride side or the groom side

Things to check before event

1. The stage decoration - it should be as per the theme decided by us including diyas or fresh flowers or artificial flowers etc. whatever is finalized.
2. Sitting arrangement of the people should be such that stage is visible from every side.

3. You can have chairs covered with clothes to look decent.
4. Dining area should be sufficient to accommodate the public all at one time.
5. The round table should be set, with chairs around with neat and clean table cloth.
6. The dining area should be well lit up.
7. The stage height should be such that its not too high nor too low.
8. The stage lighting and photographer should be well placed so there is no reflection and complete coverage of the dance performance is done from end to end.
9. Mic should go all along the stage from the left most point to the right most point.
10. In case of fire crackers, it should be placed properly on stage so they don't turn upside down and blast in a wrong direction.
11. Check the mic volume and its disturbance prior, also check the speaker quality and it's location place in the area so you get the feel of a musical Night from every location
12. Check the pendrive to be attached, there should not be any discrepancy at the last moment
13. All songs should be in sequence in pen drive and in different folders, also coordinate and explain that to the DJ player.
14. Finalize the sequence of performance and convey those to participants as well as to the DJ player.

15. In case of an anchor, the complete story line should be discussed in detail with her/him.

16. The photographer should be shown all the near and dear ones of bride and groom so he can make the coverage accordingly.

17. For pre sangeet photography assign one hour prior, so accordingly set your beauty parlour timings.

18. Dressing should be such that it is comfortable to dance, specially the footwear should be very comfortable.

19. In case of garba in the end, leave good space between stage and audience so that the seating arrangement should not be changed later on and everything is visible clearly.

20. The entry of the couple should be well planned with nice decoration on the walkway so there is no confusion at the last moment.

21. The firecracker should be placed all along tje walkway to get the best effect.

22. In case of winters, heater should be placed at intervals so that temperature of the area is comfortably maintained.

23. For dining, the live counter should be placed such that public of two live counters doesn't clash.

24. One person per table should be available to bring food for people.

25. In case of ring ceremony a ring plate and a cake with a cake table should be ready when it is announced.

This event is usually kept so that bride's and groom's family and relatives can have an informal introduction before the wedding. Earlier no such event used to be organized because marriage was usually conducted amongst the members of the same gnayati so people used to know each other but now marriage is conducted in unknown families so introduction function is necessary.

Ganesh sthapan/ Mandap muhurat

1. Usually these muhurats are early in the morning so you need to get ready early, decide the time for beauty parlour accordingly.
2. Chandarvo is tied over the front door of the house. Puda of ghas(dried jowar stems are placed in it)
3. Pooja is done for chandarvo.
4. For Ganesh Sthapan idol of Ganpati is required.
5. The pooja samagri needs to be brought by Brahman or you which is pre decided.
6. The basic things required are
   two or three bajot for Idol
   2 patla seat for parents
   Kanku, abil, Gulal, halder, Sindoor and Chokha one mindhal, manek sthambha.

1 napkin, 2 plates, 1 tapeli,1 spoon
nagarvel na pan, nadachadi, dharo, shrifal,
5 asaniyas, 2 Diya- ghee, cotton
Fruits, dry fruit, panchamrut and milk.
more detail is to be given by the Brahman

7. The Dholi needs to come early to play the Dhol, finalise the time with him half an hour before ganesh sthapan.
8. Manek stambh is required along with one bucket full of mud, 5 elders of the house put this in the bucket full of mud.
9. Total 7 matlis are required, 4 big one, 3 small one, 7 kodiyas, and 7 dhaknas.
10. One basket of mud is required.
11. Pooja of these matlis is done with Kanku and Chokha
12. Dholi takes you to take matliwala and brings back with dance.
13. Lagna Pado is to be given to the groom by bride side well before the wedding day.

Any pooja or any pious event is started by invoking Ganesh first and so Ganesh sthapan is the first vidhi in the series of vidhis proceeding. Matli is a symbolic representation of Brahmand. 3 small matlis are placed one over another near Ganesh sthapna on the base of whole wheat. The rest 4 are done pooja and placed near gotraj. Gotraj means the first ever rishi out of saptarshi whose descendants we are. So this matli is kept as a memoir of our ancestor. During Navratri this matli is perforated and a diya is kept inside it as a symbol of shakti. After ganesh sthapan and matli poojan mandap muhurat is done. Mandap is a temporary shelter constructed at the doorstep. Adorned with colorful curtains and frills it gives a feeling of excitement and joy. Today decorator does this job of constructing. In earlier times gents of the kutumb(paternal cousins) used to do this job. Today a symbolic Maneksthambh(a small wooden pillar with four arms and a small pyramid structure at the top) is done pooja and planted in a pot of mud.

Mindhal (a seed to be tied at the bride and groom's wrist). If at all bride or groom is poisoned then this seed is immediately crushed and eaten by the them to avoid the effects of the poison.

After this Pithi or Haldi rasam is done.

Pithi/Haldi

A beautiful stage backdrop of yellow colour with fresh flowers makes it look elegant

1. If pithi is to be done together (bride and groom's) than two kamal pots are required or else only one.
2. It should have one bajot inside to sit.
3. Keep ready Kanku, Chokha to start with the Tilak
4. 4 Haldi sticks decorated with cotton dipped in kanku is encircled on head of

bride/groom and thrown in 4 different directions.

5. For pithi, one can use turmeric cream or
6. One bowl with Pithi ready mix needs to be kept ready.
7. 4 Kumari girls should be made to sit in four corners of groom or boys in case of bride. Prepare a bowl of Ghee and gud and give a small morsel of it to each four and the bride/groom.
8. Coordinate the timings with photographer to cover complete event
9. Keep fresh flowers handy to pour on bride/groom.

Pithi or Haldi is a ritual performed on the bride or groom. Pithi is a mixture of haldi, perfume, chana flour. This paste is applied on whole body of bride and groom so that their skin becomes shiny and smooth. This is basically to improve skin tone to look beautiful to attract each other. Ladies of the kutumb apply haldi to the bride or groom with singing songs.

Gujarati culture is rich with wedding songs for each event of the wedding. But today this art of singing wedding songs is diminishing because it is not getting passed to young generation. Actual participation of kutumb's females by singing different songs on different events makes the function very lively and exciting. All these songs are very meaningful. They indirectly preach the importance of marriage, how the bride should behave in her new house, how should the other members of the house behave with the new bride, what is the importance of other professionals of the society like kumbhar, maali, goldsmith, copper vessel vendor, mochi, dholi, Suthar, ironsmith etc.

Grah Shanti/ Mameru

3 bajot for deity / sthapan
2 bajot for parents
1 for bride or groom
6 asaniya's for every bajot Hawan Kund, Lakda, Hawan samagri, ghee
The basic Pooja samagri is required
Kanku, abil, Gulal, Haldar, Sindoor and Chokha,
2 plates, 1 tapeli, 1 spoon nagarvel na pan, nada chhadi, dharo
2 napkins
Fruit, dry fruit, panchamrit, dudh
In between comes Mameru

1. Dholi plays the music with his beats to make people dance on his notes
2. 5 - 6 decorated chabs are carried by mamas and mamis with a wedding dress, jewellery, chappal, sweet, dry fruit etc
3. When Mameru comes at home it is welcomed with Kanku Sathiya and Chokha and then showed to family members.
4. Juice / cold drink and starter is served during grahshanti which is followed by lunch.

5. The photography of an individual and family photos is planned before or in between when people are fresh.

6. In Mameru bride's mama gives wedding saari, blouse, chaniyo(panetar), wedding chappals, some gold jewellery, silver judo, anklets, foot rings for the bride and some gold jewellery for the sister and money cover for sister's husband.

Grahshanti is a ritual to pacify all grahas(horoscopic planets). Marriage is a major Sanskar of all the 16 sanskars in sanatan dharma. Each Sanskar creates an emotional maturity in an individual. When all these vidhis are performed with shloka chanting it creates an atmosphere where negative energy drives off. A sense of responsibility for the future life is created. It creates emotional transformation. Usually Grahshanti is performed by bride/groom's parents. All nav grahas are pacified by their pooja and a havan is done wherein a shrifal is given as a offering to the God. In this pooja bride/groom also joins in. When this pooja is near completion, bride/groom's maternal uncles and maasis' families come along with jewelry for their sister and bridal costume set for the bride/groom. This is given as a gesture of participation in the joy of their sister and to remind that relation with the brothers is still live and important. Gifts brought by the brothers is then welcomed with doing pooja and accepted.

Jaan prasthan

1. Time should be decided calculating other Timings, so plan beauty parlour sittings accordingly.
2. Jaan prasthan is usually at grooms home in case of same city.
3. In case of different city, bus booking is must and time should we calculated accordingly.
4. Photographer should be called on time at home for the photos of the individual and the family at home.
5. Posh bharvanu at home in presence of Ganesh sthapan
   1 shrifal, White cloth, 5 kg of chokha, 5 coins , 5 sopari are required.
6. 4 sisters hold the cloth on four corners and one sister places chokha(rice) and shrifal which is then given to groom's Foi.
7. Do darshan of Ganesh sthapan, bow down to elders, dada Dadi and deity of the home.
8. Sister does the tilak to the groom with Kanku and chokha and garlands the groom.
9. One shrifal is given to groom while leaving home. All the near relatives offer sweet water (sugar water) to the groom/bride when the bride is leaving home for wedding venue.
10. Damru(one small metal container in which small pebbles are filled and covered with

metal lid and decorated) is given to sister to play the music.

11. Dholi is called and people can do the Garba while leaving the home.
12. Provision of number of cars to take all people to the wedding destination should be done and people should be informed how they will reach there at baraat start poin.t
13. Take dry tissue in your handbag to rub the sweat of the groom.
14. The starting point and time of the Baraat is decided as per Hast melap time. Usually one hour time is considered for baraat and so keep the start point near the venue and the time for start as 1.5 hrs prior to hastmelap time.
15. Groom's mother should not forget to take along, Gharcholu (red saari for bride) mangalsutra, cheda chedi cloth and antarpat cloth at the wedding place and a money cover for Juta hiding, foot thumb holding, to be given to bride's brothers and a cover for groom's sister who will stop the car before driving home after marriage. Pallu(or the jewellery, which is called stree dhan) which is to be given to bride can be given just before wedding or can be given 2 to 3 days earlier.
16. Bride's mother should take along money covers for the immediate relatives given as gift (called shikh), varmala, two fresh flowers garlands, gold gift to be given to

daughter as kanyadan, gold gift to be given to groom (chedo pakadvanu),5 gifts to be given to ladies who wishes "akhand saubhgyavati" to bride,(3 from groom's side and 2 from bride's side), Purat(vessels to be given to bride), a steel box (laadi kachora no vadko), raman divo(symbolic lamp) and napkins at the wedding place.

17. If possible, keep a security guard at the house when you all leave for the Jaan and house is locked to avoid thefts.

Vidhi for proceeding for marriage signifies that now when you enter the house you will not be alone. Your wife will be there with you, whose care you have to take life time. The purpose of flowing Akshat(rice) behind the groom's back is that Akshat gives positive energy to the groom. Sweet water is given to the bride/groom so that he does not feel thirsty on the way to bride's place.

Baraat

1. People should gather at one decided place where the band is called, it should be approximate 500 m to 1 km away, not more than that.
2. If in case you wish a ghodi then book it prior and ask him to come at a specific location.
3. In case of car, car needs to be decorated with a flower bouquet in front and back.

4. Music testing should be done half an hour prior of the start time.

5. Police permission needs to be taken for taking Baraat on road, you get this from respective area's police station at the given date and time.

6. Keep few 10 rs notes spare to give to musicians.

7. Final Garba needs to be done in front of the gate and ask the bride people also to join.

Jaan Agman

1. Once the jaan is on gate, bride's family needs to be present to greet them.

2. Brides mother needs to be present.

3. 1 bajot for groom and sampoot (two kodiyas joined tied by nadachadi) should be there so that the groom crushes the sampoot with his right foot and then steps into the mandap.

4. Bride's mom needs to wear khes and modh with a copper lota in her hand filled with water.

5. Kanku, chokha and Aarti Thali needs to be ready for the pooja of the groom.

6. Wet wipes , drinking water or juice and some dry fruit or starter should be served when the Jaan is coming in.

When the baraat reaches the bride's mandap the groom is made to halt there. Bride's mother comes to Ponkhva(one sort of vidhi to welcome the groom , drive away the evil spirits and najar utarvanu). There are 4 wooden small bars having different shapes called ponkhanas. They are ghunsari,musal, ravai, traad, and 4 idi pindi which are thrown in 4 directions to keep away the evil spirits. Four ponkhanas are things used in farming indicating that husband and wife should now dig the sansar, sow seeds, water them, and harvest the fruits of the sansar. After this vidhi, bride comes to welcome the groom by garlanding him at the mandap's entry. The groom then puts his manhood to the test by crushing the samput by his right leg indicating he is powerful to face any obstacles in dual life which is now going to start.

Wedding

The checklist needs to be cross checked before commencement of wedding.

1. Decoration part of the walkway, Chori, sitting chairs, dining area should be well analyzed and all set with cleanliness.
2. Taste the food before starting the serving, check out the number of items as decided in the menu and check the number of dishes told to the caterer. Always give 10% less figure of your expected guests to avoid overpayment of unused dishes.
3. Check out the items of chori - Hawan Kund, 2 chairs, 2 stools or other chairs, 2 bajot, 2 patla and complete Pooja samagri

as per the talk with the Brahman needs to be ready.
4. Valet parking Counter should be near the gate.
5. Photographer and video grapher should be assigned their locations on chori and ask one photographer to move in the ground and dining area because bride's parents are busy with the pooja and they will not know who all had come for the wedding. Its only in the photographs that guest's visit is captured. Sometimes this photographs may help in searching thief if any occurred.
6. Provision of generator needs to be checked

Once the jaan enters, please offer

1. Drinking water, wet wipes , dry fruit, mouth freshner, tissue, sweets.
2. Make the Jaan sit in a specific covered area so people can refresh.
3. Guide them the washroom which needs to be neat and clean.
4. Start serving the starter.
5. Take the groom to the groom's room, allow him to refresh, place few water bottles, tissue, nasto, sweets and everything else which is required.
6. In case of couple photography, take time for it no.

7. Let the pooja start in the chori parallely for Kanyadan, parents of bride will do that.
8. Keep 2 napkins on side to wipe hands.
9. Send an invite to the groom to come to the chori. In some cases the groom directly enters the chori and takes his place.
10. Once the puja goes on, make the bride ready.
11. If the bride needs to come with Dholi, pomp and show then plan it accordingly .
12. Chunari covering is required over the bride, it can be of fresh flowers with four brothers holding four corners of chunnari and bride walking in centre.
13. Chori light points should be checked before by photographer and video grapher.
14. Antar pat is to be brought by groom side.
15. Cheda Chedi cloth and varmala are to be brought by bride's side. Two fresh flower garlands
16. Time for hast melap should be managed to keep the muhurat.
17. Gharcholu and mangalsutra is to be brought by groom side
18. Jamai chhedo chodavani gift is to be brought by bride side.
19. Akhand Saubhagyavati gift is to be brought by bride side.
20. Purat
    matlu, 1pavali, sweets, 6 Thali vadki chamachi gifts

5 sarees are to be brought by brides side and given to the groom side

21. Money covers are to be kept ready for Juta, pag no angutho pakde aeno behen barnu roke aeno, - all by groom side

22. 4 brothers of bride are required for pheras to put chokha in the hand of bride.

23. Bride and groom goes to the brides home/or where Ganeshsthapan is done, do darshan of Ganesh sthapan and Pooja there and play Eki Beki i.e. Kanku colored water is filled in a wide vessel and some few coins, supari and silver foot ring is kept. Five chances are given. Bride and groom collect as many items they can in their palm and for 3 times husband asks wife are the items in odd numbers or even numbers. If the answer is correct then that party wins. In the last chance foot ring is to be found. One who gets it is the winner and it is believed that person will rule the house.

24. Hands of bride and groom are put in Kanku Thali and imprinted on wall/cloth and then both of them comes back to the hall

25. During vidai - One cover is kept ready for sister who stops the car before moving, Brahmin does the pooja of tyre of car and shrifal is placed under the tyre of the car/bus and crushed into two pieces. One piece is given to bride to take alongwith her in a steel box.

26. Bags of bride needs to be transferred to the grooms car.
27. One bag is to be packed differently which the bride and the groom would be taking to the hotel after wedding.
28. Pancholu is setup and family of both sides sit for dinner.
29. At the time of bidai a ramandiya,(symbolic of lamp) is given in bride's hand and bride's mother gives her modh(a crown like head band) to groom's mother indicating that now it's her responsibility to take care of her daughter.
30. After vidai, bride and groom reach to the groom home, do darshan of Ganesh sthapan there and do the required Pooja
31. They play aeki beki in one plate full of kanku water and one ring is immersed in it which is needed to be found.
32. Bride then unknots the cheda chedi and now they are free to move separately.
33. Then bride and groom goes to the hotel removing the Jewellery at home.
34. Take one bag - the bag should contain the night wear, makeup remover, tissue, wipes and dress for the next day along with the Jewellery.
35. Next day there is pag phero of the bride, Bride's sister/brother goes to bride's new home and brings her to mayka/parent's house, they have lunch and then bride goes back to her new home along with groom, A money cover and 500gm of dried khajoor

(kharek), and dried coconut is given in daughter's hand as they visited home for first time after wedding.

Wedding vidhi:

After the groom enters the mandap he directly goes to the chori and occupies his chair which is facing east. Chori is a square place. Stacks of matka (metal or other decorative) or sugarcane stems are placed in the four corners. This place indicates God's vivah place. The groom and the bride represent Lord Vishnu and Lakshmi in the chori and so their seat is at higher level than the bride's parents. Bride's father washes groom's foot and mother washes bride's foot. Father then places bride's right palm on groom's right palm indicating I am giving my daughter's hand to you, now you are responsible for her happiness and livelihood. This is hastmelap. Then bride and groom both put garland on each other's neck and commit life long partnership. Three females from bride side and two females from groom's side murmur 'akhand saubhagyavati' in bride's ears.

In the mangal phera Bride and groom hold hands alongwith the thumb and in first 3 pheras bride is ahead and in the last one groom is ahead. Bride's brother gives Akshat in bride's hand which are offered in the havan kund. In the first phera she prays Aryam dev to allow her to go to her husband's home.(Dharma's phera). In the second phera she prays for long life of her husband (kaam) and in the third phera she prays for wealthiness of her husband (arth). Each time she touches a supari (symbolic of stone) kept at one corner by her right foot thumb for strong commitment. In the fourth phera (moksha) husband is first and wife follows. Husband then touches his foot thumb to the supari and bride's brother holds his leg. He asks for groom's commitment for strong and stable marriage life for his sister and for this groom gives gift in return for the commitment.

Then in saptpadi wife holds husband's foot thumb and touches seven suparis and in the same way husband also does the same. At each touch they promise each other the seven pillars of successful and stable marriage life.

Seven wows of husband: step forward to attain Aishwarya, second step for shakti, progress in life in third step, desire for happiness in the fourth step, for kalyan of animals, fifth step, happiness according to season in the sixth step and for eternal friendship take seventh step.

Seven wows of wife: first step;you have given me saubhgya, I promise to take care of your family, I will cook best meals, I will remain Pavitra ,wear saubhagya symbols and will please you, I will be partner in joy and sorrow and will not appease any other male, I will not cheat you,I will follow as per your wish to attain dharam, arth and kaam and in the presence of all I have accepted you as my husband and I submit my body and mind to you. In this way oaths of saptpadi is taken. After that kansar bhakshan vidhi is done. In that husband and wife offers kansar (sweet) in each other's mouth.

Mangalsutra is a chain having black beads. It is a symbol of marriage. Likewise sindur applied in head is also a symbol of married woman. This is done to protect the woman from other male's malacious intentions.

Bride and groom then leave their fingerprints on the wall of bride's house or on cloth if ganesh sthapan is done elsewhere as a proof of marriage when marriage certificate was not a reality.

Now is the time for bidai. Bride's mother gives raman divo in the hands of the bride indicating this will help you to find out ways in your future life and the modh is now given to groom's mother indicating that now its your responsibility to nurture the bride.

The wheel of the vehicle in which the couple is driving home is then made pavitra by doing its pooja and sacrificing a shrifal there. Shrifal indicates that your life may be hard but always try to churn out sweet water from it. Bride's mother wishes safe journey to the couple and all the baraatis.

When the couple now enters groom's house, groom's mother rotates a kalash filled with water to move away evil spirits. Then the couple sits near the ganesh sthapan, plays eki beki , unknots each other's mindhal, and groom's sister unknots the cheda chedi to free them from the rituals.

The new life now begins.

Reception

This is the last event of the wedding, it is completley organised from the grooms side.

The checklist to cross check before the reception commences

1. Check the stage decoration, it should be as per finalized with proper usage of lightings and flower. The back of the stage should not have any decoration at the head level because it disturbs the decent photography. All bouquets and flowers should be high above the head level.
2. Check the walkway decoration, it should be well lit, neat and clean with no wires coming in between.
3. Valet parking counter should be kept near the gate so it is convenient for all.
4. The dining area should be neat and clean and well lit and decorated.
5. Taste every food item before starting it to serve

6. The live counters should be separate and highlighted so that they are visible clearly and there is no hustle among the people.
7. The stage and the steps going up and down needs to be sturdy, covered with a carpet
8. One flower line should be kept near the stage edge for better photography.
9. Set proper location of photographer and videographer, at a proper height to capture the best view of the reception stage.
10. Keep a broad sofa of big chairs for the couple so that you can put gifts behind them which cannot be visible to guests and in photography.
11. Assign the responsibility to collect all gifts and money covers to your relative to put it safely in non-decorated car to avoid thefts from stage and cars.

General suggestions

1. During the full wedding process to make it comfortable keep one morning and

evening cook, one or two helpers at home and one driver.

2. Make a list of all agencies with their contact number on one sheet of paper and give zerox of it to few family members so that in case of some confusion they also can solve the problem. Make a group wherein phone number of all agencies like, caterer, decorator, brahman, music band, dholi, matliwala, beauty parlour are saved.

3. Finalize the cost with every agency and put it on the paper to set your budget.

4. To make it convenient, write down all the things discussed with every agency and make a diary for the record .

5. Also make a new file, keeping all the receipts of the advance payment and the full payment for your record to get the total at the end of the event and to make the remaining payment.

6. Jewellery purchasing, dress purchasing, and the things to be purchased for the girl are completely your choice and I have not discussed it in this book. Save all the bills of purchases for any exchange in future.

7. While calculating the number of dishes to be said to the caterer - reduce 20% of the total invitees and give the number to avoid wastage of dishes in wedding and reduce 10% of total invitees and give the number for other events.

8. Save all the bills of gold purchases and write on it for whom that item was

purchased. This helps you for future reference and in any incometax raid.

9. Keep a diary wherein all money rituals are written right from engagement to wedding/reception. Write down all the gifts you receive for all future references.

10. For an average wedding to decide the budget classify your expected expenditure under different headings like:

Clothings, jewellery, beauty parlour(with mehndi for all events), gifts to be given, wedding day(decorator, caterer, music band/dholi, florist, bus, hall rent ghodi), other events like haldi, sangeet, bhajan (hall rent, decorators, caterers, choreographers), photography(for all events). This will help you as a reference for your other child's marriage.

Wish you a successful, enjoyable and memorable wedding.

----------------------The End--------------------